TEN KEYS FOR
UNLOCKING THE BIBLE

TEN KEYS FOR UNLOCKING THE BIBLE

*Treasures That Will
Change Your Life*

Colin S. Smith

MOODY PRESS
CHICAGO

Moody Press, a ministry of Moody Bible Institute,
is designed for education, evangelization, and edification.
If we may assist you in knowing more about Christ
and the Christian life, please write us without obligation:
Moody Press, c/o MLM, Chicago, Illinois 60610.

Interior design by Kelly Wilson, Paetzold Associates,
St. Charles, Illinois.

ISBN: 0-8024-6547-1

3 5 7 9 10 8 6 4 2

Printed in the United States of America

For ten special friends
who are key partners
in unlocking the Bible:

Bill Bradish, Randy Davis,
Ruth Guillaume, Gary Griffin,
Bob Hansen, Steve Hiller,
Dick Nordman, Mickey Ryg,
Bill Thrasher, and Russ Williams.

PHILIPPIANS 1:4–6

CONTENTS

INTRODUCTION

You are holding a small book that will give you the big picture of the Bible story. The Bible is the world's best-selling book, but it is long and sometimes difficult to understand. This book will give you a place to start. It's rather like a high-altitude flight over a range of mountains. You'll see what the ground looks like and get a good glimpse of the highest peaks.

The whole Bible is one story. It begins in a garden, ends in a city, and all the way through it points us to Jesus Christ.

The "keys" will open up the story of the Garden of Eden, where God introduces Himself and tells us who we are. We'll learn about the disaster in the garden and its effects on our lives today. Then we will follow the Old Testament story, discovering how right through human history God has been reaching out to men and women, making a way for us to know Him, and inviting us to come.

The "keys" will also open up the story of Jesus, exploring His birth, death, and resurrection. We will discover who the

Holy Spirit is, and see what God intends the church to be. Then we will take an honest look at the Christian life: the struggle that every Christian experiences and the power that God makes available to us. Finally, we'll take a glimpse at the highest peak of all—the new creation that God has promised when Jesus Christ returns in glory.

It has again been a pleasure to work with the publishing team at Moody Press on this project. I am also deeply grateful to Greg Norwine and Tim Augustyn who serve with me on the pastoral staff at Arlington Heights Evangelical Free Church in Illinois. They had the idea for this book and have provided the questions for reflection at the end of each chapter.

The "Ten Keys" are condensed from *Unlocking the Bible Story*, a series of four books that cover the story in greater detail. If you enjoy the high-altitude flyover and want to get closer to the ground, *Unlocking the Bible Story* will give you a map and a compass. There's so much more to discover.

But for those who are new to the Bible or want a quick overview of the Christian faith, this is the place to begin.

Join me on the journey. You're in for some breathtaking views.

The
GARDEN

—DISCOVER—

who you are and why your life matters to God.

—LEARN—

why this world is not as God made it.

—WORSHIP—

because Jesus has opened the way back into God's blessing.

*T*HE first thing Adam knew, he was staring into the face of God.

God had formed his body from the dust of the ground, but it lay there lifeless, like a corpse until God breathed into it. Then Adam became a living being (Genesis 2:7), and in his first moment of conscious existence, he knew that his life had come from God.

God is invisible, but right from the beginning of the Bible story, He has been reaching out to make Himself known. That's why He made Himself visible to Adam. We call this a "theophany," an appearance of God in visible form. It was God's way of creating a relationship.

God introduces Himself as our Creator and therefore our owner. He made you in His image (1:26), and you are of unique value to Him. God chose to bring you into being. He did that on purpose, and you will discover that purpose as you get to know the One who created you.

THE GARDEN OF EDEN

The Bible tells us that "the LORD God had planted a garden
in the east, in Eden; and there he put the man he had
formed. The LORD God took the man and put him in the
Garden of Eden" (2:8, 15).

We cannot be certain about the garden's location, but it is
important to grasp that it was a real place. It was located
near the Tigris and Euphrates Rivers (2:10–14), which run
through modern Iraq.

God prepared a place for Adam, and God put him there.
He does the same thing for us. The Bible says that God has
determined the exact places for all of us to live (Acts 17:26).

The place where God puts you will not be perfect. Even
Eden was exposed to the possibility of evil. But there is no
better place to be than where God has set you down. You
are not where you are by accident but by the plan and the
purpose of God.

God gave Adam the responsibility of naming the animals
and caring for the garden (2:19). Work is a good gift from
God, and God took pleasure in what Adam was doing. It
may be hard for you to imagine that God would enjoy the

documents you prepare, the components you assemble, or the home you create . . . but He does.

A MARRIAGE MADE IN HEAVEN

The LORD God made a woman from the rib he had taken out of the man, and he brought her to the man. *(2:22; EMPHASIS ADDED)*

I'd love to have seen the expression on Adam's face! God appeared to Adam and said, "Adam, I have someone I want you to meet!" I have no doubt that Adam's jaw dropped wide open. He certainly seemed pretty pleased! He said, "This is now bone of my bones and flesh of my flesh" (2:23).

God brought them together. Try to picture that in your mind. The LORD God takes her hand and puts it into his hand and says, "Here is the partner I have made for you!"

When two people marry, God does in an invisible way what He did for Adam and Eve in the garden. If you are married, try to picture God taking your hand and the hand of your spouse and joining them together. When you know God has joined you together, it will help you weather the most difficult times.

A Loving Command

God came into the Garden of Eden as a visitor, making Himself known and cultivating a relationship with the man and the woman. He did not impose Himself on them but gave them the opportunity of choosing a relationship of faith and obedience with Him.

God gave Adam a single command that was, like all His commandments, a wonderful expression of His love. "You must not eat from the tree of the knowledge of good and evil, for when you eat of it you will surely die" (2:17).

God had made everything good, and so "good" was the only thing that Adam knew. The purpose of God's command was to keep him from evil.

The Origin of Evil

The Bible does not give us a full explanation of the origin of evil, but it does tell us where it started. Alongside the visible world that we know, God made an invisible creation in heaven and filled it with angels.

The devil was one of these angels. He became inflated with pride and tried to usurp the position of God (see Isaiah

14:12–14). His rebellion was unsuccessful and led to his being excluded from the presence of God and cast down to the earth. So right from the beginning of human history, there was an enemy bent on destroying the work of God. His first aim was to introduce the man and the woman to the knowledge of evil.

RECRUITING FOR THE REBELLION

Satan came into the garden with the aim of recruiting the human race into his rebellion against God. Spirits are invisible to us, and so when Satan wanted to communicate with the first man and woman, he came in the form of an alluring serpent. He presented himself as a friend and began to question the single commandment God had given.

"Did God really say, 'You must not eat from any tree in the garden'?" (Genesis 3:1). If Satan could create confusion in Eve's mind about what God had said, he would be well on the way to gaining power over her.

Then Satan suggested that God had exaggerated the consequences of sin. "You will not surely die" (v. 4). In effect, he said, "How could you possibly believe that a single act of disobedience would lead to something as drastic as death?"

But his third suggestion was the one that tipped the scales
for Eve, and her husband. "God knows that when you eat
of it your eyes will be opened, and you will be like God,"
he said (v. 5).

Adam and Eve decided that they wanted this knowledge of
evil. They disobeyed God's single command and they got
what they wanted. We have all lived with it ever since.

HOPE IN A CURSE!

> *The LORD God said to the serpent, . . .*
> *"Cursed are you." (3:14)*

When a person or thing is "cursed," it is consigned to
destruction. So when God cursed the serpent, He was
announcing that evil would not stand. When God spoke
about a Deliverer who would crush the serpent's head,
Adam and Eve must have been overjoyed (v. 15).

A CURSE DEFLECTED

> *To Adam he said, . . ."Cursed . . ." (3:17)*

Adam must have held his breath. God had cursed the serpent, and now He was looking straight at Adam as He spoke
that ominous word again.

Adam must have thought that he would be utterly destroyed, but he was in for a surprise. Instead of saying to Adam, "Cursed are you," as the LORD did to the serpent, God said, "Cursed is the ground because of you" (3:17).

God deflected the curse away from Adam so that it fell on the ground and not on him directly. God kept His judgment away from Adam, creating room for future reconciliation. On the day he sinned, Adam discovered the grace and mercy of God. The curse that should have been on him went to another place.

OUT OF EDEN

Our first parents were banished from Eden (3:23), where they had known the blessing and presence of God. Life became a struggle in a hostile place, where they were exposed to all kinds of danger from wild animals.

Over time, they would notice lines and wrinkles in their skin. They would experience pain and discover that the "death" God had spoken about was a terrible reality that they could not avoid.

God placed cherubim—angels representing His judgment and holiness—at the entrance to the garden, along with a flaming sword flashing back and forth, barring the way to the Tree of Life. It must have been a terrifying sight.

The Shattered Sword

Try to imagine yourself standing with Adam and Eve outside Eden, looking back at the angels and the flashing sword of judgment. There's no way back for you into the presence of God. If you tried, the sword would cut you down.

But as you look, someone comes out from the presence of God and stands beside you. Then He turns and advances toward the flaming sword. You cringe as you look. The sword is flashing back and forth, and you can see what will happen to Him when He gets there. But He keeps walking forward, steadily, and relentlessly.

The sword strikes Him . . . and kills Him. It breaks His body, but in breaking His body, the sword itself is broken. The sword that killed Him lies shattered on the ground. By His death, the way back to the presence and blessing of God is opened.

That's what happened when Jesus died. The judgment that keeps us out of God's presence struck Him. It was spent and exhausted on Him. The sword of God's judgment broke itself on Him, and so the way back into God's blessing is wide open for all who will come.

Pause for Prayer

Almighty God,

*I acknowledge You are my Creator and owner. I thank You
that You have made me in Your image. I want to come to
know You better.*

*I recognize that You are the only One who can deliver from the
power of evil. I see that the world needs to be delivered from
evil, and I acknowledge that I need to be delivered from its
power in my own life, too.*

*Thank You that Jesus Christ has come into the world so that evil
will not stand. Thank You that, by His death, He opened the
way back into Your blessing and into Your presence for all who
will come. May I be one of these people.*

In Jesus' name, amen.

Questions for Discussion

1. What have you inherited from your parents for which you are thankful?

2. What difference does it make if you were created by God or are a product of evolutionary forces? What are the implications of each?

3. Can you remember a situation where you felt guilty and genuinely were? How did you deal with your feelings of guilt?

4. God desires each of us to regain the life our first parents enjoyed in the garden. What would have to happen to make that possible?

GOD continued to give good gifts to our first parents, but outside of Eden, their struggle with evil intensified. When Eve held her first son, Cain, she must have hoped that he would be the deliverer God had promised. But he killed his brother and became the world's first murderer. As the generations advanced, evil multiplied and people knew little about the living God.

But God would not abandon the human race. He appeared to a man called Abraham, promising to bless him and, through him, people from every nation on earth (Genesis 12:1–3). From that point on, the Bible follows the story of Abraham's descendants.

At the height of a famine in Canaan, Abraham's grandson Jacob moved with his family to Egypt. The migration saved their lives, and over the next four hundred years, the people God had promised to bless grew from a large family to a nation of almost two million people.

As they grew in number, the Hebrews were oppressed and became slaves. God raised up Moses and, despite the determined resistance of Pharaoh, delivered them from Egypt. God brought them into the desert at Sinai and made a covenant with them. They would be His people and the Lord would be their God. Then God gave them the Law . . .

CHAPTER 2 —— EXODUS 20

The
LAW

—DISCOVER—

life's ten greatest struggles and how to prevail in them.

—LEARN—

how the Law brings us to Jesus Christ.

—WORSHIP—

as you see how Jesus turns God's commands into promises.

$\mathcal{M}$OSES was shaking as he stood at the bottom of the mountain surrounded by two million terrified people. As they looked up, they could see "Mount Sinai . . . covered with smoke, because the LORD descended on it in fire" (Exodus 19:18). The whole mountain shook as the God who walked with Adam in the garden came down.

The people were so terrified that they asked Moses to go up the mountain so that God could speak to him. They could not bear to have God speak with them directly. So Moses climbed the mountain, and God gave him the Ten Commandments (20:3–17).

A GLIMPSE OF THE GLORY OF GOD

The Ten Commandments are not an arbitrary set of rules. They are a direct reflection of the character of God.

When God said, "You shall have no other gods before me" (20:3), it was because He is the only God. There is no one else like Him.

When He commanded that we rest on one day each week, it was because He rested on the seventh day of Creation.

Why should you not commit adultery? Because God is faithful.

Why should you not steal? Because God is trustworthy.

Why should you not lie? Because God is truth.

Why should you not covet? Because God is at peace and content in Himself.

The Law reflects the glory of God, and if our lives are modeled on who God is, this is what they will look like.

THE GREATEST BATTLES OF YOUR HEART

The Ten Commandments also identify the greatest struggles of human experience.

In the first commandment, God said, "You shall have no other gods before me." We don't find it easy to let God be first in our lives. Like Adam and Eve in the garden, we want to take the place of God ourselves.

In the second commandment, God said, "You shall not make for yourself an idol." We struggle to worship God as He is and prefer to think of God as we would like Him to be.

When God said, "You shall not misuse the name of the LORD your God," He was saying, "You will be tempted to use my name to support your own prejudices and express your own frustrations," and when He said, "Remember the Sabbath day by keeping it holy," He was telling us that we would have a battle over giving Him our time.

The first four commandments reflect our struggle to love God with our whole heart. The last six commandments speak to our struggle to love our neighbor as ourselves.

When God said, "Honor your father and your mother," He identified our difficulty in submitting to authority.

We also struggle with issues of ongoing hostility. God speaks to these in the sixth commandment: "You shall not murder." Christ tells us that the issue here goes beyond physical violence to the underlying resentment we may feel toward others (see Matthew 5:21–22).

In the seventh commandment, "You shall not commit adultery," God tells us that that there will be a battle for sexual purity. Again, Christ made it clear that this commandment speaks to the difficulty of keeping our minds and our thoughts clean.

Then, there is a battle for personal integrity—"You shall not steal"—and a battle for honesty—"You shall not give false testimony against your neighbor." There will be circumstances in which you will be inclined to exaggerate a story, to misrepresent the way things are, or simply to tell a downright, barefaced lie.

Finally, we struggle over this whole business of contentment. That's why God wrote the tenth commandment: "You shall not covet." When you see what other people have, it will create within you a feeling that you should have it, too.

These are the battles of our lives; are they not? They are the great struggles that we all face in some degree or another. The Law is like a light shining into our souls, and when we look at what God says to us, we have to admit that He is speaking directly to the primary battles of our hearts.

An X Ray of the Soul

I went to see the dentist recently. I'd been putting it off for a long time mainly because I had no pain. The experience was not encouraging.

My dentist took some X rays and then held them up to the light. "Mmmm . . . Oh dear! . . . Nasty. There's a lot of decay underneath these fillings," he said.

"I've no pain," I insisted. But he didn't seem impressed. "You're going to need some pretty major work," he said. "And the sooner, the better."

Many people go through life with no sense of pain over their spiritual condition. They make the false assumption that things are well with them and that, having lived generally respectable lives, they are in good spiritual shape. But God's Law is like an X ray to the soul. It shows us that we are people who find it difficult to let God be God, and that it is natural for us to love ourselves more than other people.

The first reason you need Jesus Christ is not that you'll have a richer, fuller, and more satisfying life. It is that you are a sinner by nature and by practice. The X ray of God's Law shows it.

The Law is a good thing, just as X rays are good, even if they bring us bad news. I didn't like the bad news at the dentist, but I was grateful to know about the problem before it got worse. If you don't know there's a problem, you won't pursue the remedy.

The Law is like a teacher to bring us to Christ (see Galatians 3:24 NLT). When you learn what the Law has to teach, you will come to Jesus Christ.

LAYING TRACK FOR THE TRAIN

The Old Testament story makes it clear that God's people were not able to keep His Law. The Law tells us what to do, but it doesn't give us the power to do it.

Later in the Bible story, God promised a new covenant in which He would not only tell us what to do, but give us the power to move in that direction. "I will put my Spirit in you and move you to follow my decrees and be careful to keep my laws" (Ezekiel 36:27).

God's Law is like the rails for a train. The rails give direction, but the train will not go anywhere unless there is power in the engine. It is the special work of the Holy Spirit to give God's people power to move in the direction that is laid out in God's Law.

TURNING COMMANDS INTO PROMISES

There's a great story about a man serving time in prison because he was a thief.[1] Stealing had been his lifestyle, until the long arm of the law caught him. During his time in prison, he heard the good news of Jesus Christ and was wonderfully converted.

When the time came for his release, the man knew that he would face a new struggle. Most of his old friends were thieves, and it would not be easy to break the patterns of his old way of life.

On the first Sunday of his new freedom, he slipped into a church building. The Ten Commandments were inscribed on a plaque at the front, and his eyes were immediately drawn to the words of the command that seemed to condemn him. "You shall not steal."

That's the last thing that I need, he thought to himself. *I know my weakness. I know my failure, and I know the battle I'm going to have.*

As the service progressed, he kept looking at the plaque. As he reread the words, they seemed to take on a new meaning. Previously he had read them in the tone of a command: "You shall not steal!" But now, it seemed that God was speaking these words to him as a promise: "You shall not steal."

He was a new person in Christ, and God was promising that the Holy Spirit would make it possible for him to overcome the habit of stealing.

God's promise is that when you believe in the Lord Jesus Christ, the Holy Spirit will come and reside in your life. His power will make the difference between a battle in which you are destined for defeat, and a battle in which there will be ultimate victory. The Law tells us how God wants us to live. Christ makes that life possible.

 *Pause for Prayer*

Which of the Ten Commandments speaks to the area of your greatest struggles right now? Take a moment to identify the commandment, and then ask God to make this an area of victory for you by the power of His Holy Spirit. As you pray, remember the promise of Romans 6:14: "Sin shall not be your master."

Holy Father,

Thank You for giving the Law to reveal the extent of my sin and show my need for a Savior. You know I continue at times to struggle with [name the sin] and have broken Your commandment.

I recognize that I need Jesus Christ and thank You that He has come to deliver me from the power of sin in my life. Give me victory in this area [name it] by the power of the Holy Spirit.

It is in Christ's name that I pray, amen.

Questions for Discussion

1. On what basis should a parent decide the rules their children must follow?

2. Why do you think God chose these ten commandments?

3. Which of the Ten Commandments do you think are the most difficult to follow? Why?

4. In this chapter we learned that the Law is like an X ray. What is this X ray revealing about the condition of your soul?

NOTE
1. I heard the story from my friend Charles Price and am grateful for his permission to use it. See Charles Price, *Matthew* (Fearn, Scotland: Christian Focus, 1998), 88.

GOD'S people became tired of waiting for Moses and persuaded Moses' brother, Aaron, to make an idol. Then they indulged in a wild party to celebrate the new god they had made for themselves. So even while God was giving His laws to Moses at the top of the mountain, the people were busy breaking them at the bottom.

God does not impose Himself on people who do not want Him. He told the people that they could go into the land of Canaan where they would enjoy freedom and prosperity, but He would not go with them.

To their great credit, the people then recognized that the presence of God was more important than freedom and prosperity. But how could God's presence return to people who had so obviously sinned against His Law?

Over the next seven months, the people followed God's instructions for building the tabernacle. This was a mobile worship center, separated into different areas by a series of curtains, and containing various pieces of symbolic furniture.

At the center was an area called the Most Holy Place. On one day in each year, the high priest was to go there and offer a sacrifice. Then, God promised, His presence would come down . . .

The SACRIFICE

—**DISCOVER**—
the great drama of the Day of Atonement.

—**LEARN**—
the gospel from God's greatest visual aid.

—**WORSHIP**—
as you see how Jesus fulfills the role of our great High Priest.

$\mathcal{I}$F you ever find yourself in a court of law, you probably will want to hire an attorney to present your case. Law courts are intimidating places, and they operate under some fairly complex rules, so you need the help of an attorney to represent you before the judge and speak on your behalf.

In the Old Testament, the priests did something similar in the presence of God. They operated in a mobile worship center called the tabernacle.

At the center of the tabernacle was the Most Holy Place, which was screened off from view by a heavy curtain. Inside was the ark of the covenant. It was a wooden chest, carried on poles, with a lid on top. Rising from the lid were two golden figures of cherubim—angels representing the judgment of God—who had guarded the entrance to the Garden of Eden. Between these two figures was an area known as the "atonement cover" or the "mercy seat."

God had said that He would meet with the high priest in the Most Holy Place on the Day of Atonement that was celebrated once a year (Leviticus 16:2; Exodus 25:22).

A FIVE-ACT DRAMA

God often teaches us through pictures, and the Day of Atonement is His greatest visual aid. It is like a drama in five acts, each one pointing us forward to Jesus Christ, and it helps us to understand the significance of His death on the cross as the sacrifice for our sins.

Act 1: The Priest Appears

If you saw the high priest, you would immediately have known that he was one of the most important people in the land. His magnificent robes displayed the dignity of his office.

But on the Day of Atonement, the high priest discarded his robes and appeared in the streets wearing a simple white cloth. People would line the route as he made his way toward the tabernacle like a boxer entering the ring.

Act 2: The Priest Prepares

Before the high priest could enter the presence of God to offer a sacrifice for the sins of the people, his first priority was to deal with his own sins. He took the blood of a slaughtered bull into the Most Holy Place; and sprinkled it on the mercy seat.

Act 3: Atonement Is Made

Then two goats were brought forward, and one was slaughtered. The high priest took its blood behind the curtain and sprinkled it on the mercy seat, between the two golden figures of the cherubim that represented God's judgment. Justice was satisfied and mercy was released when the sacrifice was made.

Just as in the garden, God had diverted the curse away from Adam and onto the ground; so now, God was ready to allow the death sentence to be passed on an animal instead of the sinner.

Act 4: Sin Is Confessed

What happened next was the most dramatic part of the whole Day of Atonement.

The live goat was brought forward. God had instructed the high priest to "lay both hands on the head of the live goat and confess over it all the wickedness and rebellion of the Israelites" (Leviticus 16:21).

During child dedication services, I have often struggled to offer a coherent prayer as a wriggling two-year-old tried desperately to escape my clutches. But such problems are nothing compared with what the high priest had to do here. He had to confess all the sins of Israel while holding onto a live goat with both hands!

The high priest identified specific sins in his prayer, and if you had been in the crowd, you would have recognized some of the sins he confessed as your own.

As the high priest prayed, an act of transfer took place. The guilt of these sins was removed from the people and laid on the goat. The high priest "put them on the goat's head" (v. 21). So at the end of his prayer, there was one very guilty goat!

Act 5: Guilt Is Removed

Then God told the high priest to "send the goat away into the desert in the care of a man appointed for the task" (v. 21).

Imagine the scene as the goat is led away, between the tents and then outside the camp and into the desert. You watch until the man and the goat are only a dot on the horizon, and then you cannot see them at all.

I cannot imagine a more powerful visual presentation of the gospel. This five-act drama was like a dress rehearsal for the real performance that took place when Jesus Christ came into the world. It was like a preview, telling us what to look for and what to expect when He came.

A NEW FIVE-ACT DRAMA

Run forward through fifteen hundred years of history and you move from the dress rehearsal to the opening night, from the preview to the main event, featuring Jesus Christ in the role of the High Priest.

Act 1: Christ Appears

In the New Testament, another high priest appears. He is not a son of Aaron like all the others: This Priest is the Son of God! His glory is far greater than the splendid clothes worn by the high priest. He shared the glory of the Father before the world began. But just as the high priest discarded his magnificent clothing on the Day of Atonement, so Christ laid aside His glory and took the form of a servant. He was wrapped in strips of cloth and laid in a manger.

Act 2: Christ Prepares

Jesus did the will of the Father and fulfilled all the work that the Father had given Him to do. He was what every other priest wished he could be. He lived the life that no other high priest was able to live. His perfect life qualified Him to achieve what all the other high priests could only illustrate.

Act 3: Christ Makes Atonement

After three years of His public ministry, Jesus was arrested and sentenced to be crucified. On the cross, He became the sacrifice for our sins. The judgment of God was diverted away from us and onto Him. When His blood was shed, God's justice was satisfied, and God's mercy was released.

Act 4: We Confess Our Sins

This is where you have a part to play in the drama. Just as the high priest laid both hands on the head of the live goat and confessed the sins of the people, God invites you to "lay hold" of Jesus Christ in an act of faith and confess your sins to Him.

The sacrifice offered by Jesus is sufficient to cover the sins of the whole world. But it is not until you come to Him in faith and confession that His sacrifice is applied to your sins in particular. Have you done that?

When you do, God counts the guilt of your sin as being transferred to Jesus Christ. It is laid on Him and included in the sin for which He died.

Act 5: Our Sins Are Removed

When our sins have been laid on Christ, God promises that He will take them as far from us "as the east is from the west" (Psalm 103:12).

Try to imagine a person who has been struggling with a troubled conscience. Let's call her Sarah. She has made a foolish choice and wonders if God can ever forgive her.

Sarah is in the crowd watching the great drama of the Day of Atonement. The following day, she is still struggling with her conscience when a friend comes to talk with her.

"Sarah, think about what you saw yesterday. What happened when the high priest grabbed that goat by the head?"

"He confessed our sins."

"And did he confess your sin?"

"Yes, he did, and when he spoke about it, I felt so ashamed."

"What happened to the sins that he confessed?"

"They were laid on the goat's head."

"And what happened to the goat?" her friend asks.

"It was taken away."

"How far was it taken, Sarah?"

"Farther than I could see."

Take that picture and apply it to your own life. Can you picture your sins being taken away into the distance and out of sight? God wants you to know that, through the finished work of Christ, your sin is forgiven and your guilt is removed.

Pause for Prayer

Gracious Father,

Thank You that the Lord Jesus Christ has come into the world to be my High Priest. Thank You that He was willing to lay aside His glory and to be born in a manger. Thank You for His perfect life that qualified Him to make atonement. Thank You that He has made atonement by laying down His life and shedding His blood.

I believe in the Lord Jesus Christ and, right now, trust in Him as my Savior and Lord. I confess my sins to You . . . [Take time to confess your sins to the Lord.]

Thank You that Christ died for these sins. Thank You for taking these sins from me. Help me now to enjoy the peace of knowing that You have taken them as far from me as the east is from the west, through Jesus Christ my Lord, amen.

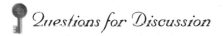 ## Questions for Discussion

1. If you had been in the crowd on the Day of Atonement, what would have impressed you most?

2. If Billy Graham or Mother Teresa had been the high priest/ess, each would have needed to make atonement for his or her own sins before bringing others' sin before God. On a scale of 1–10 (1 being sinless, 10 being completely evil), where would you put each of them? Where would you put yourself?

3. What kind of a case could you make for your innocence before God's Law?

4. What would you have felt if you had been in the crowd on the Day of Atonement when the goat disappeared over the horizon?

*A*FTER forty years in the desert, God led His people into the promised land of Canaan. God's presence was with His people: He raised up leaders in times of crisis and gave the people victory over their enemies. But the people noticed that other countries had kings and standing armies, and they wanted to be the same.

The first king, Saul, was a disappointment, but under the leadership of his successor David, God's blessing was evident. David brought the ark of the covenant to the city of Jerusalem; he wanted the worship of God to be at the center of national life. God promised that one of David's descendants would establish a kingdom that would never end, and that He would reign forever.

It wasn't David's son Solomon. In his later years, Solomon turned away from the Lord, and when he died, the kingdom divided in two. Ten tribes in the north separated from the line of David. They suffered under bad leadership until the northern kingdom was overrun in 722 B.C.

Two tribes continued in the south. Some of their kings honored God; others led the people into evil. God spoke to the kings and the people through prophets who heard the Word of God directly as Abraham and Moses had done before.

One of these prophets was Isaiah. God told him to issue an extraordinary invitation . . .

The INVITATION

—DISCOVER—

*the amazing auction in which what is offered
goes to the lowest bidder!*

—LEARN—

how Christ can satisfy the deep thirsts of your soul.

—WORSHIP—

because God offers His good gifts to all who will receive.

*I*N the town where my wife, Karen, and I used to live in north London, market day was every Thursday and Saturday. Crews would arrive at around six in the morning and set up the scaffolding and the canopies for the stalls.

There were stalls with fruit and vegetables, a luggage rack, clothing stalls, and a man who strangely seemed to do nothing but sell parts for vacuum cleaners. The place was always milling with people looking for a bargain.

God uses the picture of a marketplace to explain His incredible offer to us:

> *"Come, all you who are thirsty, come to the*
> *waters; and you who have no money, come,*
> *buy and eat! Come, buy wine and milk without*
> *money and without cost." (ISAIAH 55:1)*

Centuries later, Jesus took up these words and applied them to Himself. "If anyone is thirsty," He said, "let him come to me and drink" (John 7:37). Thus the street trader of Isaiah 55 is the Son of God. He offers to satisfy the deep thirsts within your soul. Let's go over to the stall and discover more.

The Price Is Right!

"Come, buy . . . without money and without cost." (v. 1)

Selling is usually about the trader arguing the customer up to his price, but here we have Christ arguing the price down! It's like an auction in reverse where everything is turned on its head, because Christ has chosen to sell to the lowest bidder.

So come with me in your imagination to this auction sale! Christ is standing in the stall, and He says, "I am pleased to be able to offer total forgiveness and reconciliation with God. The offer includes the ultimate value of everlasting life, and it is available today to the *lowest* bidder."

A man in a pin-striped suit steps forward with the first bid. "I've led a good life and run an honest business," he says. "I have been faithful to my wife and have been a good father to my children. I have served on the boards of three charitable organizations. I would like to offer these good works."

A murmur rises from the rest of the bidders. That's a pretty impressive offer. "It's with the man in the pin-striped suit," says the auctioneer.

Then a lady in a blue coat lifts her hand. "I haven't done as much as the man in the pin-striped suit," she says, "but I have attended church faithfully, and I think that I have become a spiritual person."

"It's with the lady in the blue coat," says the seller. "Can anyone make me a lower offer?"

A girl in blue jeans raises her hand. "I haven't attended church like the lady in the blue coat, but I am sincere in wanting to do what is right, and I have tried to live a life that is pleasing to God."

"Well," says the auctioneer, "that's not very much, but it's going to the lowest bidder, so you have it. Am I hearing any other bids?"

A man in a red sweater, with a bit of a red face to go with it, gets up slowly. "I've not lived up to my own expectations," he says, "I have let people down, and I've done some terrible things, but at least I have been sorry. I didn't intend to do what I did, so let me offer the fact that I am truly repentant."

"Well," says the seller, "that really isn't much. But it's going to the lowest bidder, so your meager bid has it right now. Is anyone going to make me a lower offer?"

This is not a battle of pride; it is a battle of blushes. Many people have opted out of the bidding, not because the cost is too high, but because the offers are embarrassingly low. Most people are just watching to see if anyone would dare to offer less than the man in the red sweater. How could anyone offer so little to God?

Finally someone steps forward and says, "I don't have anything to offer. My repentance isn't what it should be; my faith isn't what it should be; my works aren't what they should be. Nothing is as it should be! I have nothing to offer."

And the auctioneer brings down His hammer. "It's yours," He says. "It's yours."

WHAT DO WE BRING?

Maybe you're saying, "OK, but don't we have to bring something to God? Don't we have to be sorry? Don't we have to believe?"

Yes. But we do not receive salvation because we offer these things. Salvation is a gift. Many people become confused at this point. They think of salvation as a deal in which God offers forgiveness and life, and we bring repentance and faith, and somehow we get together and make the trade. But that's not the gospel.

The blind man did not come to Christ because he had sight; he came to Christ to receive sight. You do not come to Christ *with* a changed life; you come to Christ *for* a changed life. You come to Christ to receive.

If God were to ask you on the last day why He should let you into heaven, the answer is not "because of my good works" or "my repentance" or even "my faith." Our salvation does not rest on anything we have done. It rests on Jesus Christ alone.

If we are trusting in our repentance and faith, we will never have assurance, because our faith and our repentance are never what they might be. Our salvation depends entirely on Christ. Faith is the open hand that receives what He offers, and repentance is the response of a heart that has received.

OFFERING THE LOWEST BID

Many people have difficulty in worship because they have never received what Christ offers. They are following a moral code and offering that to God. In fact all that they have ever done is offer things to God. Their hands are full, and they have never come to Christ to receive.

God has made it so that every one of us can make the lowest offer. Only pride stands in your way. The man in the pin-striped suit and the lady in the blue coat may have this blessing also, but they must stop trying to buy it. They must lay aside their works and come to Christ empty-handed.

Of course when we do that, it leaves us incalculably in debt to Jesus for the rest of our lives. We look up into the face of Christ and say, "I cannot even express the debt I owe for what You have given me. So I will worship, love, and obey You for the rest of my days; not so that I may receive, but because I have received."

MAKING THE PURCHASE
"Come, buy." (v. 1)

Having established that salvation is a free gift, Christ now invites us to come and buy. He uses the word *buy* because there is a definite transaction in which you take what Christ offers. Even though you do not pay for it, you must receive it, and unless this transaction takes place, what Christ offers to you remains, as it were, in the stall.

LOOKING ISN'T BUYING

Some people enjoy "just looking" in shops, and there is absolutely nothing wrong with that. That's where some people are spiritually. They have come over to Christ's stall and started asking questions about the Bible and salvation.

Looking is great, but looking isn't buying. The greatest commitment of your life is worthy of the deepest investigation, so look into the claims of Christ carefully. But don't confuse looking with buying. If what Christ offers is to become yours, you must close the deal.

TRYING ISN'T BUYING

If we had bought every dress my wife has tried on over the last twenty years, we would be truly bankrupt! But trying isn't buying. You could be in a store from nine until five, Monday to Friday, and never buy. And you can come to church, read the Bible, join a study group, and still never close the deal with Christ. You can feel that you should buy and still never buy.

KNOWING ISN'T BUYING

We were looking at washing machines a few months ago.
We did our research and found a brilliant sales assistant.
He was like an encyclopedia of washing machines.

"This one," he said with a rather nasal voice, "rotates with
twenty-three minutes of agitation; and this one has the
corkscrew spindle, but it does not have the automatic
temperature gauge."

We began talking with him, and eventually he told us that
he didn't own a washing machine himself because he lived
on his own, had plenty of socks, and went to the laundry
once every month. He knew all about the products but had
never bought one himself. We didn't buy the washing
machine either.

Maybe that is where you are spiritually. You have learned
many things about Jesus, but what He offers has not yet
become yours. Knowing isn't buying.

There's a time for doing your research, but if you are going
to buy, there must come a point where you make a decision
and close the deal. And when you buy, what Christ offers
becomes yours.

Christ says, "Come, buy, without money, without price."
Are you ready to buy?

Pause for Prayer

Almighty God,

Thank You that Jesus Christ has come and purchased the gift of reconciliation and everlasting life with You. Thank You that He offers this gift to me freely.

Forgive me for my pride in thinking that there was something I could offer in payment for such a gift. Humbly I acknowledge that I have nothing to offer You. My hand is empty, but it is open to receive.

Gladly I receive what You freely give, amazed that what You purchased at such cost may so simply become mine.

Words cannot express the debt I owe. Fill my heart with Your love and lead me into Your paths. Let me live for Your glory, through Jesus Christ my Lord, amen.

Questions for Discussion

1. In the auction analogy, we imagined people offering different "bids" to be exchanged for forgiveness and eternal life with God. What "bids" do you think most people are counting on in order to get to heaven?

2. What is the acceptable "bid" to gain God's forgiveness and entrance into heaven? Why?

3. Why is it hard for us to accept that salvation is a free gift? What must we admit about ourselves and our lives in order to come to this conclusion? (For a hint, see Isaiah 64:6 and Romans 3:10–12.)

4. Where are you in the purchase process right now—looking, trying, knowing, ready to buy, or already made the purchase?

THE STORY CONTINUES...

$\mathcal{N}$OT many of God's people listened to His invitation. From the time of Isaiah on, most of them resisted God's commandments and shaped their beliefs and behavior to their own liking. As they abandoned faith in God, evil multiplied in the land. Corruption, greed, and violence were rife.

God continued to speak to His people through the prophets, warning them that if they did not turn from idols and wickedness, He would remove His blessing and give them into the hands of their enemies. As time went on, God's warnings became more specific. But nothing changed.

In 586 B.C., the Babylonian army destroyed the city of Jerusalem. Many died, a few fled, and the rest were taken as exiles to Babylon. It was there that some of God's people began to repent and seek Him in a new way.

After seventy years in exile, a small community returned to the ruined city of Jerusalem. They restored the city walls and built a new temple. But the cloud of God's visible presence did not come to the new temple as it had before.

The people must have longed that God would come to them. But nothing remarkable happened for over four hundred years until one night, a baby was born . . .

The MANGER

—DISCOVER—

*why Jesus is different than any other person
who has ever lived.*

—LEARN—

the significance of the virgin birth.

—WORSHIP—

because God has come to us in Jesus Christ.

*I*MAGINE that you are living on a large and beautiful island, and that your home is on a sandy beach beside the ocean.[1]

The islanders are all descended from castaways who were washed up there after a great disaster many years ago. Many of the islanders know little or nothing about it. In fact, most modern islanders do not believe that anything exists beyond the horizon.

At the center of the island is a high mountain with what looks like a crater at the top. Some people say that it is a volcano. But the horrendous scenarios predicted by some have never happened, and most people have come to the conclusion that they never will.

MESSAGE IN A BOTTLE

One morning, as you are strolling on the beach, you discover a green bottle that has been washed up on the shore. Inside there is a message: "Help is coming."

Strange. What kind of help could you possibly need?

A few weeks later, you see another bottle with a similar message. "Help will arrive soon!"

The discoveries are strangely unnerving. After all, you are living on an idyllic island and are enjoying a very full and satisfying life. But the notes in the bottles keep suggesting that you are in some kind of danger.

You decide to tell your neighbor Bill.

"Bill, have you seen any green bottles on the beach?"

"No. Why?"

"Well, a few days ago I found one with a note inside. I didn't think much about it, but then I found another with the same message. Somebody is out there beyond the horizon. They are telling us that we are in some sort of danger, and they obviously have some kind of plan to help us."

"Oh, that sounds rather fanciful to me," says Bill. "The notes were probably written by kids farther round the island. If they threw the bottles out to sea, it's quite possible that the tide washed them back in. You don't want to worry about a few messages in a bottle!"

But somehow you can't get the bottles and their message out of your mind. "Help is coming."

HELP WILL COME

The story of the islanders can help us grasp the Bible's message. After our first parents sinned, they were "cast away" from the presence of God, and we live in a world that, for all its beauty, has a curse hanging over it. The problem we face is not about finding fulfillment on the island; it is that the whole island will be destroyed.

But God has promised that help will come. That is why Jesus Christ came into the world. He came from the "mainland" of heaven. The Bible tells us how it happened.

GOD TAKES THE INITIATIVE

> God sent the angel Gabriel to Nazareth, a town in Galilee, to a virgin pledged to be married to a man named Joseph, a descendant of David. The virgin's name was Mary. (LUKE 1:26–27)

The angel announced that Mary would "be with child and give birth to a son" (v. 31). But Mary could not see how this could possibly be, given the fact that she was a virgin (v. 34).

The angel's answer takes us to the heart of the greatest and most wonderful mystery in the whole Bible.

> *"The Holy Spirit will come upon you, and the*
> *power of the Most High will overshadow you.*
> *So the holy one to be born will be called the*
> *Son of God." (v. 35)*

The Bible contains other stories of miraculous births. The birth of Isaac, when Abraham and Sarah were both well past the age of conceiving children, was a miracle. But God worked through the union of a father and a mother. Both Abraham and Sarah were involved.

This was different. Mary was a virgin. Joseph had absolutely nothing to do with the child she bore. Not only did he have no union with her before the child was conceived, but he had no union with her until after the child was born (Matthew 1:25).

God was taking the initiative. Jesus did not arise from the human race. God sent His Son to the human race. God the Son became a man, taking flesh from the Virgin Mary.

The New Testament teaches three foundational truths about the identity of Jesus: (1) He is God; (2) He is man; and (3) He is holy.

THE INCREDIBLE JOURNEY

Your life began when you were conceived in your mother's womb. Before that moment you did not exist. God used the union of your father and your mother to bring you into being. Before that, you were not, and without that, you would not have been.

But with Christ, it is different. His life did not begin in the virgin's womb. Before He was born in the stable, He shared the life of God.

The apostle Paul tell us that Christ was in very nature God, but He "did not consider equality with God something to be grasped." Instead, He "made himself nothing, taking the very nature of a servant, being made in human likeness" (Philippians 2:6–7).

That's why the angel told Mary that her child would be called the "Son of the Most High" (Luke 1:32) and "the Son of God" (v. 35). He is "God with us" (Matthew 1:23).

Does the Bible's claim that Jesus is God with us matter?

Absolutely. It is of great importance, because only God can reconcile man to God. Salvation has to be from the top down. Suppose you are adrift in a dinghy and you need to be rescued. Someone who is secured to the helicopter is lowered on a winch. As you embrace him, you are lifted with him to the position from where he came. Salvation is from above. Only God can save.

Christ came on an incredible journey from heaven to earth, and in Him God reaches out to every person.

HE'S REALLY ONE OF US

Once we have grasped that Jesus is God, it is every bit as important for us to grasp that He is a man. On several occasions in the Old Testament, God appeared in a visible form. But these appearances were only temporary. They could be compared to an actor dressing up or putting on a disguise.

But the birth of Jesus is entirely different. The Son of God took human flesh to Himself. He did not cease to be God, but He became a man.

Everything else in the New Testament revolves around this one miracle. If God became man in Jesus, we should not be surprised at His claims, His miracles, or His resurrection. In the words of Dr. James Packer, the Incarnation is, in itself, an unfathomable mystery, but it makes sense of everything else that the New Testament contains. Once you know who Jesus is, it all begins to fit.

As C. S. Lewis pointed out, "We believe that the sun is in the sky at midday in summer, not because we can clearly see the sun (in fact we cannot) but because we can see everything else."[2]

Does the humanity of Jesus matter?

Absolutely. The fact that Jesus is a man is as important to our salvation as the fact that He is God. Only man can bear the punishment of man's sin. The Son of God became one with us so that He could stand in our place under the judgment for our sins. This is why He was given the name Jesus, because He would save His people from their sins (Matthew 1:21).

A NEW KIND OF HUMANITY

"The holy one to be born will be called the Son of God." (LUKE 1:35; EMPHASIS ADDED)

Jesus Christ was like us in every respect except one. He is holy. This means that He did not at any time commit a single sin (Hebrews 4:15). But it means more than that. He is holy in His thoughts, in His intentions, and in His character. His nature is holy.

The holiness of Jesus opens up a whole new world of hope for us. We have become so used to fallen humanity, that it is difficult for us to imagine a human being who is not subject to sin and its consequence—death. "To err is human," we say, as if erring were inseparable from being human.

But Jesus blazes the trail of a new humanity that will be holy—free from sin and no longer subject to death. This has always been the purpose of God.

That's what Jesus was talking about when He said, "I have come that they may have life, and have it to the full" (John 10:10). This is the life that He offers to you. He has come to lead us into a holy life. For those who believe, that journey begins now and it will be complete in heaven. When we see Him, we will be like Him (1 John 3:2).

Pause for Prayer

Gracious Father,

Thank You for sending Your Son into the world to become my Savior. Thank You that He is fully God so that He is able to save, and fully man so that He is able to save me. Thank You that in Him I may be reconciled to You.

I confess that I find it too difficult to imagine any other world than this one. But I believe Your promise that this world is passing away and know that my life in it is short. Thank You that Christ has come to bring me into a new life.

I trust Him to make me holy and to bring me into Your presence. Thank You that He has become like me so that I may become like Him. I pray in His name, amen

Questions for Discussion

1. The message in the bottle said, "Help is coming." Why do we need help?

2. If Jesus were a man but not God, what difference would it make?

3. Jesus came to make us holy. If you were holy, how would you be different?

4. If Jesus could change your life, would you want Him to?

NOTES

1. Adapted from a story in Eugene Peterson, *Working the Angles* (Grand Rapids: Eerdmans, 1987), 139–44. Peterson adapted his story from an essay by Walker Percy, *Message in a Bottle* (New York: Farrar, Straus, and Giroux, 1975).

2. C. S. Lewis, *Miracles* (Glasgow: Colins, 1947), 114.

THE STORY CONTINUES...

*J*ESUS began His public ministry at about age thirty. His message was very simple: "Repent, for the kingdom of heaven is near" (Matthew 4:17). God was opening up access to heaven, and inviting people to submit to His rule.

Wherever Jesus went, He did good. He taught the people with authority, and His miracles revealed His power and glory. He was able to subdue the ravages of nature, to deliver distraught people from the power of demons, and to heal diseases. On three occasions He brought someone who had died back to life (Luke 7:11–17; 8:41–42, 49–56; John 11:1–44).

As news about Jesus spread, opposition increased. Many found His claims threatening, and some began a plot to have Him killed. This did not take Jesus by surprise. He told His disciples that He had to go to Jerusalem to suffer and die. He also told them that, on the third day, He would rise again, but they did not understand what He was talking about.

One night, a large crowd armed with swords and clubs came to arrest Him. A show trial followed in which false witnesses spoke against Him. The Roman governor should have upheld the process of law, but instead, he asked the people what should be done with Jesus. They called for Him to be crucified. So Pilate handed Him over . . .

The CROSS

—**DISCOVER**—
what Jesus accomplished in His death.

—**LEARN**—
how Paradise has been opened.

—**WORSHIP**—
because nobody is beyond the reach of God's mercy.

I HAVE a friend who went to live with a primitive tribe in northern Thailand. Having gained acceptance, he built a home in their village and began to learn the language. The tribal people worshiped their ancestors. My friend went there to tell them the good news of Jesus Christ.

I asked him how he went about explaining the gospel in a way that these people would understand. "It's very simple," he said. "We tell them the Bible story."

He began by explaining who God is and how He made the world. He told his listeners the story of how their first parents were driven out of the garden, and then he took them through the Old Testament story, explaining the Law, the sacrifices, and God's promise to send a Savior.

"You have to explain the framework before they can understand the message," he said.

BUILDING THE FRAMEWORK

Postmodern America is very different from the jungles of Thailand, but we encounter some of the same problems in communicating the gospel. There was a time in this country when most people had a working knowledge of the main stories of the Bible. But that is no longer the case.

If we are to explain the Christian message clearly in our culture today, we must tell the whole story. It is not enough to say, "God sent Jesus to die for our sins," because that won't mean much to a person who doesn't know who God is, what sin is, or why somebody dying would make a difference.

That's why we studied the stories of the garden, the Law, and the sacrifices. We've learned that sin leads to death, but God accepted the death of an animal instead of the sinner. God builds all this into our minds so that we can understand what was happening at the cross.

The cross is God's answer to the problem presented in the Bible story. When we grasp the scale of the problem, we will be able to see the magnificence of the solution.

Jesus hung on the cross for six hours. What happened during these hours of unrelieved and excruciating agony takes us to the heart of the Bible story.

FORGIVENESS IS RELEASED

When they came to the place called the Skull, there they crucified him. (LUKE 23:33)

Man's sin reached its full horror and its most awful expression at Calvary. Not only had we disobeyed God's commandments and defied God's name, but now we were crucifying God's Son.

I sometimes wonder what must have gone through the minds of angels as they watched what was happening on that cross. They had gasped in wonder when they saw the Son of God take human flesh as He was born into the world. Now they saw that flesh torn by a whip, a crown of thorns being embedded in His head, and nails piercing His hands and feet.

If there was ever a moment in human history when God's judgment had to fall, this was it. But Jesus cried out, "Father, forgive them, for they do not know what they are doing" (v. 34).

Christ knew that God's judgment would come, but He was saying, "Don't let it fall on them; let it fall on Me, and on Me alone. Let Me be the lightning rod for Your judgment on their sin. Allow Me to be the sacrifice that is consumed, but don't let Your judgment fall on them."

Just as God had spared Adam when the curse fell on the ground, so now God spared those who stood round the cross, as His judgment for their sins fell on Jesus.

This is the heart of the gospel. Jesus stands under the judgment of God for our sins. Christ asks the Father to divert the punishment away from us, and He absorbs it in Himself. That is how forgiveness is released.

When Christ prayed, "Father, forgive them," His prayer included the priests who condemned Him, the crowds who mocked Him, and the soldiers who crucified Him. But it extended further. It also included the disciples who deserted Him and the Old Testament believers who had waited for Him.

His prayer covered the sin of every person who would come to Him. And if His prayer could cover the sins of those who nailed Him to the cross, then it will cover every sin you have committed or could commit.

PARADISE IS OPENED

A few feet away from Jesus hung a man who had made a tragic waste of his life. Having pursued a life of crime, he had faced human justice and was now, himself on a cross, paying the price. Soon, death would relieve his suffering, but then he would enter the presence of God where he would face divine justice. His position seemed hopeless.

He turned painfully toward Jesus and said, "Jesus, remember me when you come into your kingdom" (v. 42).

He did not know much about Jesus; indeed, a short while earlier he had joined with his colleague on the other side of Jesus in ridiculing His claims. But as death drew near, something changed. He seemed to have a new awareness of how awesome it would be to enter the presence of God. Ridiculing Jesus no longer seemed appropriate. "Do you not fear God?" he said to his friend.

He had heard Jesus praying, "Father, forgive them." Perhaps Christ could forgive him too.

> Jesus answered him, "I tell you the truth, today you will be with me in paradise." (v. 43)

Paradise! This man's life had been a series of disastrous choices, but Jesus promised him an immediate translation, through death, into a life of undiluted joy.

The awful suffering that he was enduring would soon be past, and then he would enter eternity. But he would not face the condemnation of God, because Jesus was taking that for him.

Before the day was over, Jesus would usher this man into the presence of God. Suddenly this man, for whom the world held nothing, found that because of Jesus he was about to enter the greatest joy a human being can ever know.

When Jesus died, the way back to God's presence and blessing was opened for all who will come.

THE SUN STOPPED SHINING

It was now about the sixth hour, and darkness came over the whole land until the ninth hour. (v. 44)

Jesus had suffered the judgment of men. Now He would endure the judgment of God. As Jesus entered into the heart of His sufferings, God kept the sun from shining.

Christ entered all the dimensions of hell while He was on the cross. In the hours of darkness, He bore our guilt, endured God's wrath, and suffered the taunting of evil. He endured all this alone without the comfort of His Father's presence. In the depth of His suffering, He cried out, "My God, my God, why have you forsaken me?" (Mark 15:34). No words can express the depth of His suffering.

But then, the darkness passed. The storm was over. The judgment poured out on Christ was exhausted, spent. Justice had been satisfied. At the end of the three hours of darkness, Jesus shouted, "It is finished" (John 19:30).

DEATH IS SUBDUED

All that remained was for Him to lay down His life. Jesus called out with a loud voice, "Father, into your hands I commit my spirit" (Luke 23:46).

There is a note of triumph here. He had released forgiveness and opened Paradise, as in the darkness He became the sacrifice for our sins on the cross. He had completed everything that the Father had given Him to do. The battle was over and the victory was won.

Death is like a dark valley that we all have to pass through. It is a dark place, but for the Christian it is a safe place. Christ has cleared out the enemies who lurked there, and when the moment comes for you to pass through that valley, His presence will be with you.

Pause for Prayer

Gracious Father,

*Thank You that Jesus suffered and died on the cross for me.
Thank You that He bore the sentence of death for my sins, and
that through His death Your mercy reaches me. Thank You that
He has opened Paradise, so that through His death I may enter
everlasting life in Your presence. Thank You that He was alone
in the darkness so that I should never face darkness alone.*

*I am the sinner for whom Jesus died. Gladly I trust Him as my
Savior and receive, by faith, the amazing gifts that He has purchased for me.*

Receive my worship, in Jesus' name, amen.

Questions for Discussion

1. As you read about Christ's suffering on the cross, what emotions did you feel?

2. Why did Jesus have to die on the cross? Why couldn't God simply forgive us without sacrificing His Son?

3. Two thieves were crucified next to Jesus. Why do you think one trusted Him and the other did not?

4. What do you think the death of Jesus achieved? What difference will it make for you?

THE STORY CONTINUES...

A MAN called Joseph of Arimathea went to Pontius Pilate and asked for the body of Jesus. He was a follower of Jesus, but had never openly confessed his faith for fear of what other people might think. Nicodemus, another secret disciple, came with him. Perhaps they wished that they had shown greater courage and loyalty to Him when they had the opportunity.

Pilate was cautious. His first response was to ask for confirmation that Jesus was in fact dead. The centurion confirmed the fact without reservation. Only then did Pilate release the body of Jesus.

Joseph and Nicodemus wrapped the body of Jesus in strips of linen. Joseph owned a tomb in a garden near the place where Jesus had been crucified, so they laid the body of Jesus there, and then rolled a stone against the entrance to the tomb.

The following day, Pilate ordered that a guard should be posted at the entrance to the tomb. It had been reported to him that Jesus had spoken about rising on the third day, and he wanted to make sure that the area around the tomb was secure. "Take a guard. . . . Make the tomb as secure as you know how," he said (Matthew 27:65).

They did, but the following morning was the third day . . .

The TOMB

—DISCOVER—

how the first visitors to the tomb knew that Jesus had risen.

—LEARN—

why the Christian message is not "Jesus is alive"
but "Jesus is risen."

—WORSHIP—

because Jesus Christ is risen from the dead.

*T*HE women started early because they wanted time to cherish the memory of Jesus, who had died two days earlier. Their journey to the tomb was motivated by love, but it was absolutely devoid of faith. Whatever faith they had in Christ had been overwhelmed by the darkness of Calvary. Faith was gone; all that was left was love.

Mary Magdalene, Joanna, and Mary the mother of James (Luke 24:10) were part of a group who traveled with Jesus and the twelve disciples. They had heard Christ speaking about what would happen on the third day after His death, but it is clear that on this first day of the week, they did not expect anything unusual to happen.

Many people have a deep affection for Christ, but find it hard to believe. At one time they were drawn to Christ and began to follow Him, but then they experienced great darkness in a personal tragedy or in some evil that was done, and somewhere in the darkness they stopped believing.

LOST FOR AN EXPLANATION

When the women arrived, they found that the rock in front of the tomb had been moved. When they went inside, they found that the tomb was empty. The women had absolutely no idea what to make of this. The empty tomb left them "wondering" (v. 4).

It is important to notice that they did not immediately jump to the conclusion that Jesus had risen from the dead. The first visitors to the empty tomb were quite lost for an explanation.

When they found the body was missing, Mary did not say, "I have a feeling that He must have risen from the dead," and Joanna did not reply, "You know, I have that feeling too. I think you must be right." The thought did not even occur to them.

So how did they know what happened? God told them.

GOD GIVES THE EXPLANATION

While they were wondering about this, suddenly two men in clothes that gleamed like lightning stood beside them . . . The men[1] said to them,

> *"Why do you look for the living among the*
> *dead? He is not here; he has risen!"* (vv. 4–6)

God called two angels and said, "Go and tell them what I have done. These women love My Son, but there is no way in the world that they are ever going to work out what happened. Go tell them."

Christian faith rests on believing God's explanation of what He has done.

When the Virgin Mary conceived a child, there was no way that she could have known what was happening to her. So God sent the angel to explain.

It was the same with the shepherds and the wise men. How could they possibly have known that the child in a manger was God in human flesh? Without God's explanation through the angels and the star, they would never have known what was happening.

It was the same when Jesus was crucified. Many people saw Him die, but few understood the significance of the Cross. God tells us that on a cross, Christ bore our sin, endured our punishment, and laid His life down as a sacrifice.

The women would never have worked out what had happened for themselves. God told them. Christian faith does not rest on feelings, impulses, or personal insights. It is believing God's explanation of events, given to us in the Scripture.

"HE HAS RISEN"
Risen Means That Death Is Defeated

Throughout the Bible story, death had been like a tyrant exercising a reign of terror over the human race. Nobody could escape it. "Death reigned," the Scriptures say (Romans 5:14, 17). Abraham, Isaac, Jacob, Moses, and David all believed God's promise, but death got every one of them.

When they died, they continued in a shadowy existence: separated from this life, but not able to move forward into the presence of God. Death brought them to a place where there was a way in but no way out.

When I was around kindergarten age, our school class had a pet mouse. On the weekends, each of us had the opportunity to take the mouse home.

One weekend, I was playing with the mouse along with a few toys in our home. The mouse was intrigued by my bright red, double-decker London bus and, after sniffing around, climbed inside.

This was tremendous entertainment, until the mouse reached the front of the bus. Then we had a problem. The mouse couldn't move forward, and it couldn't climb back. It was completely stuck.

I remember my father saying, "There's only one thing to do, son. We'll have to destroy the bus!" He took a knife and cut the roof open. The mouse was free.

I can't tell you what a relief that was. But my bus was never the same. It really was rather curious; a bright red London bus with half of the roof missing. Of course, this made things even more interesting for the mouse.

Before, the bus had a way in but no way out. Now, the mouse could go in the door, climb up the stairs and come out through the roof! There was all the difference in the world.

From the time of Adam to the time of Christ, death had a way in but no way out. But when Jesus Christ died, He cut a hole in death itself. For Christ's people, death is no longer a prison, but a passage that leads right into the presence of God. There's all the difference in the world.

Risen Means the Whole Person Will Be Redeemed

The message of Easter is not that Jesus is alive, but that Jesus is risen! It is worth thinking about the difference.

The Son of God was "alive" in heaven before He ever took human flesh. So why did He not simply leave His crucified body in the tomb and return to the Father? After all, it was only flesh and bone. Why did He bother with it?

The angels could still have appeared on Easter Sunday morning and said, "His body is here in the tomb, but don't worry, His spirit is with the Father in heaven." After all, is this not precisely what we say at the funeral service when a Christian dies?

The message of Easter is that Christ is risen! It was not just the spirit of Jesus that was delivered from death; it was His body.

God has joined the soul and the body together. Death separates them. That is why it is such a terrible enemy. It is the undoing of our nature. Death would not be defeated by the survival of the soul. Victory over death would only be achieved if the body and the soul were reunited in the power of a new life. That's the good news of the resurrection.

Suppose you have planned the vacation of a lifetime in
Hawaii, but just before you are due to take the trip, you
fall down the stairs and break just about every bone in your
body. In good cartoon style, you wind up in the hospital
bandaged from head to toe, with a thermometer sticking
out of your mouth.

A friend, who is a computer wizard, offers to take you on a
virtual tour instead. He sets up his laptop, and sure enough,
you see wonderful views of Honolulu. "It's so beautiful," you
say. "I just wish that I had been able to go."

"But you have," says your friend. "You have been there on
a virtual tour."

Your friend is a computer geek, so you humor him and let
him go. Whatever he says, you know that as long as your
body is stuck in the hospital, you haven't been to Hawaii.
Going there in your mind or via the Internet simply isn't
the same.

The life God promises to His people in heaven is not like a
virtual tour. It is not a spiritual experience or a mind game.
God sent His Son to redeem the whole of you, and bring
you, body and soul, into His presence. The good news is

that Christ is risen. The resurrection of the body is the glorious future that lies ahead of every Christian believer.

Risen Means We Will All Be Changed

When the body of Jesus was raised, it was also changed. This was something that had never happened before.

Jesus brought Lazarus back from the dead. It was a wonderful miracle, but Lazarus came out of the tomb exactly as he had gone into it. He carried on the process of aging at the point where he had left off, and then at some point, the poor fellow had to go through the whole miserable business of dying all over again.

But when Christ was raised, His body was no longer subject to aging or sickness. His flesh was transformed and adapted for eternity. That's why Christians can look forward to heaven. The greatest delights of body and soul in this life are only a hint of what God is preparing for those who love Him.

NOTE
1. Matthew tells us that they were angels (Matthew 28:5); Luke tells us what they looked like.

Pause for Prayer

Almighty Father,

Thank You that, when Jesus died, He changed the nature of death for all His people. Thank You that He is risen and that, by faith in Him, I will also rise. Thank You that, when Your people die, what lies ahead is far greater than what lies behind. Help me to live in the joyful anticipation of all that is to come.

Through Jesus Christ my Lord I pray, amen.

Questions for Discussion

1. God's explanation of the empty tomb is that Jesus rose from the dead. Do you believe this? Explain your reasons.

2. Some people are drawn to Jesus, but find it hard to believe. What keeps you from coming to faith in Jesus?

3. Jesus "cut a hole in death," so we have a whole eternity in front of us. What implication does this have for how you live your life today?

4. Have you thought much about death? Does it scare you? What difference does the death and resurrection of Jesus make?

THE STORY CONTINUES...

*A*FTER the Resurrection, Jesus gave "many convincing proofs that he was alive" (Acts 1:3). Putting the accounts in the Gospels and 1 Corinthians 15 together, there were at least nine different occasions when Christ appeared to the disciples, either as a group or to one or two of them individually.

On one occasion, Christ appeared to a group of more than five hundred people, most of whom were still alive at the time Paul wrote about it and were able to bear witness to the truth of His account (1 Corinthians 15:6).

At the end of the forty days, Jesus went to the Mount of Olives with His disciples. He commissioned them to go and make disciples of all nations and promised them His continuing presence. But their immediate instructions were to wait in Jerusalem. Jesus had taught them about the Holy Spirit. Now He promised that the Spirit would come.

Then Jesus ascended into heaven. The disciples saw Him go. He was taken into the cloud, which in the Old Testament represented the presence of God. He was returning to His Father.

The disciples went back to Jerusalem and waited—until the Day of Pentecost . . .

The
SPIRIT

—DISCOVER—
what God intends the church to be.

—LEARN—
the significance of Pentecost for today.

—WORSHIP—
as you see how God can use you in His kingdom.

*T*HE chairman reported that the church roll now stood at one hundred and twenty members. They had not been able to obtain a building, and so they were still meeting in a second-floor room that they had rented in the city.

There had been a good spirit at the prayer meeting and a lot of discussion about how they should fill a leadership position that had become vacant. But besides that, not a lot had been happening.

The task of reaching their community seemed to be beyond them. There was very little money, very few people, and outside of their meeting place, a culture that had very little room for their message.

That's how the church was at the beginning of the book of Acts.

But Christ had spoken about an event that would change all that. In a few days, they would be "baptized with the Holy Spirit" (Acts 1:5). Then, He said, "You will receive power . . . and you will be my witnesses in Jerusalem, and in all Judea and Samaria, and to the ends of the earth" (Acts 1:8).

They did not have to wait long. Just ten days after Jesus ascended into heaven and fifty days after the Resurrection, there was a festival called Pentecost. It was a big celebration, and Jerusalem was crammed with visitors from many countries (Acts 2:5).

On the Day of Pentecost, the Holy Spirit was poured out on the first Christian believers. After that, the church was completely different.

A SOUND LIKE THE WIND

> *When the day of Pentecost came, they were all together in one place. Suddenly a sound like the blowing of a violent wind came from heaven and filled the whole house where they were sitting. (ACTS 2:1–2)*

In the ancient world, many languages use the same word for wind, breath, or spirit. The sound of the wind is similar to the sound of breath, only it is much louder and it lasts longer.

Before Jesus ascended into heaven, He breathed on the disciples and said, "Receive the Holy Spirit" (John 20:22). Jesus was explaining what would happen on the Day of Pentecost.

So when the disciples heard a sound like the rushing wind just a few days later, they would immediately associate it with the sound of Jesus breathing on them, and recognize that this was the fulfillment of what Jesus had promised.

At the beginning of the Bible story, God breathed into Adam. A lifeless corpse lay on the ground until God gave it the kiss of life. Then Adam became a living being. The church is the body of Christ. It was like a corpse until Jesus breathed the life of His Spirit into it. God breathed life into these people, and they were never the same again.

GREAT BALLS OF FIRE

> *They saw what seemed to be tongues of fire that separated and came to rest on each of them.* (v. 3)

Try to imagine yourself among these one hundred and twenty people when this happened! What they saw must have been absolutely terrifying.

A ball of fire divided into individual flames, or "tongues of fire," that came to rest on every person in the room. The amazing thing was that none of them was burned.

In the Old Testament, God appeared to Moses in flames of fire resting on a bush that did not burn. Now, on the Day of Pentecost, God gave the same sign of His immediate presence with the first disciples. It must have been awesome.

When God appeared to Moses in the fire, He commissioned him to lead the Hebrews out of their slavery in Egypt. Now God was coming in the fire to give a new commission to His church.

Try to imagine yourself in the room when God's fire came down. Who would you have expected it to land on? Would it be Peter, James, or John, or perhaps all three? Or maybe even all of the twelve disciples?

But as the fire came down, it separated into many flames, falling on many people in the room. Imagine being there: You look up with awe as you realize that one of the flames is coming toward you. You look round at the others in the room. A flame rests on every one of them.

In the Old Testament, God gave His presence and power to some of His people. Now He was giving His Spirit to all of them. God was commissioning every believer to advance His purpose in the world.

They spoke in other tongues

> *All of them were filled with the Holy Spirit and*
> *began to speak in other tongues as the Spirit*
> *enabled them.* (v. 4)

Suddenly and spontaneously, every one of the one hundred and twenty believers found that they were able to speak in languages they had never learned.

This was a reversal of what had happened long before at the Tower of Babel. Early in the Bible story, as man's rebellion against God was gaining momentum, men built a city with a tower to proclaim their greatness and provide their security.

God came down and broke the momentum of man's godless kingdom by introducing the confusion of multiple languages for the first time into the human race (Genesis 11:1–9).

It must have been very strange. One day, a friend you have known for years talks to you, but what he is saying sounds like gibberish. Others are also making incomprehensible sounds. It's not hard to imagine what happened. People who spoke the same language were drawn together, and then the different language groups separated from each other, spread-ing out across the face of the earth.

At Babel, the tongues were a sign of God's judgment on man's rebellion. The languages brought confusion. People could no longer communicate, and so they were divided.

The Day of Pentecost was exactly the opposite. People from every nation had gathered in Jerusalem (Acts 2:5). When the Spirit of God came, the apostles found themselves spontaneously speaking in languages they had never learned, so that people from all over the world could hear and understand the good news of Jesus Christ in their own language.

At Babel, the tongues were a judgment from God leading to confusion and people being scattered. At Pentecost, the tongues were a blessing from God leading to understanding and people being gathered together.

To every tribe and nation

People all over Jerusalem heard the sound of the wind (Acts 2:6), and it was not long before a crowd gathered. When they arrived, they found the one hundred and twenty believers declaring in different languages the great things God had done.

God had determined that people from every nation and language group would hear the good news of Jesus Christ. Language would be no barrier to the gospel.

God breathed His life into the church. His presence came and rested on them as He commissioned them to advance His purpose in the world. On the Day of Pentecost a mission-oriented church was born.

People from many cultures came to faith in Christ that day, and then went back to their homes to spread the gospel among their own people so that folk from every language and culture would discover the blessing of the gospel.

WIND, FIRE, AND TONGUES TODAY

As we have studied the Bible story, we have seen several occasions when God's presence was made known in a visible way. We call these occasions theophanies, and they are always of great importance. In a theophany, God does for some people in a visible way what He does for all His people in an invisible way.

It seems to me that this is how we should understand the remarkable events on the Day of Pentecost. God is teaching us through the wind, the fire, and the languages what He always wants to do among His people.

God wants to breathe new life into His people. He does not want His church to be an inward-looking organization that functions at a merely human level, but a living body filled with the life of God.

God wants to anoint not just a few leaders, but every one of His people for ministry. The presence and the power of Almighty God rests upon every believer in the Lord Jesus Christ. And God's great purpose is that His blessing will flow through His people to all the nations of the earth.

Every Christian and every church has a part to play in this purpose. For some people that will mean going to another culture and learning another language so that the good news of Jesus may be known. For others, God's call will be to find our voice in the language God has already given us.

God puts people around every believer so that we can communicate the good news of Jesus in their language. Maybe you can speak the language of teenagers or of young children. God has wired you in a way that makes it possible for you to communicate with a certain group of people. Find out who they are, get among them, and tell them about Jesus.

Pause for Prayer

Heavenly Father,

Thank You for giving the gift of Your Holy Spirit to all Your children. Breathe Your life into me and fill me with Your Spirit. Equip me for all that You are calling me to do. Open my eyes to see the people You have placed around me, and give me courage and boldness to speak about You in a way that they can understand. Use me to advance Your purpose and to bring Your blessing to others.

I pray for Your church. May we know the life of Your Spirit among us and play our part together in bringing the good news of Jesus to the world. I pray in Jesus' name, amen.

Questions for Discussion

1. What has been your experience of the church?

2. How do you see the Holy Spirit at work in your life, small group, or church?

3. In this chapter, we learned that every Christian is empowered and gifted to serve God. How have you seen God use you in the lives of others?

4. What group of people do you feel especially able to communicate with in their "language"?

*A*FTER the Day of Pentecost, the church continued to grow. Christians were marked by an unusual joy, and their love for each other was shown by the way they shared their possessions. The church was powerfully attractive, and the lives of the early believers drew attention to the authenticity of their message.

Later, the believers faced persecution for their faith in Christ. They were scattered, and in this way the good news began to spread. God had promised that all the nations of the earth would be blessed through Abraham. The early believers were all descendants of Abraham, and through them God's promise was fulfilled as the good news of Jesus Christ began to spread around the earth.

Saul of Tarsus led the persecution of believers until God miraculously intervened in his life, bringing him to faith in Christ. The church's most bitter opponent became her greatest pioneer, and we know him better as the apostle Paul. The Holy Spirit revealed truth to Paul directly, just as

He had to the prophets in the Old Testament; and in this way the great truths of the Christian faith were committed to writing in the letters of the New Testament.

These letters were written to ordinary Christians who struggled to live out their faith in the pressures of their world. God's truth has not changed and His Word still speaks to us today . . .

The FIGHT

—DISCOVER—

why the Christian life is a winnable war.

—LEARN—

how Christ pays sin's penalty and breaks sin's power.

—WORSHIP—

because God gives the power of His Spirit to all His people.

$\mathcal{I}$T had been some years since John first used drugs at a party. He had tried a cigarette and thought he wouldn't do it again. But he did, and then some weeks later he tried something stronger. He had a hard time admitting that he was hooked, but his friends knew that was the truth.

Then one day, John was caught in possession. The police pressed charges, and the court set a heavy fine. There was a penalty to pay, but John had no money.

After a lot of heart searching, John's mother paid the fine on his behalf, but afterward she wondered if she had done the right thing. "I'm afraid that, by paying the fine, I'm just enabling him to continue his habit," she said.

She's right. John still faces the problem that he is an addict. The drugs are exercising a power in his life, and if he is to be "saved," that power must be broken.

When Adam and Eve committed the first sin, there were two long-term consequences. Sin brought a penalty against them, and it became a power within them.

So, when God saves us through Jesus Christ, He saves us from both sin's penalty and its power.

THREE CHARACTERS YOU SHOULD KNOW

In the book of Romans, the apostle Paul explains more about how God has done this. To help us understand his teaching, I want to introduce three characters. Their names are Hostile, Helpless, and Hopeful. Try to decide which one you identify with most. Then we will see what God has to say to each of them, and to us.

Hostile: No Desire and No Ability

> *The sinful mind is hostile to God. It does*
> *not submit to God's law, nor can it do so.*
> (ROMANS 8:7)

Paul speaks about a person whose mind is hostile to God. So we are going to call him Hostile.

At one time, Paul himself was Hostile. He led a furious persecution of Christian believers. He was "breathing out murderous threats against the Lord's disciples" (Acts 9:1). That's hostile!

Then, when he was traveling on the road to Damascus, the risen Lord Jesus Christ appeared to him and said, "Why are you persecuting Me?" (see Acts 9:3–6). Paul's violent anger against Christians was actually a reflection of a deeper rage against Christ.

You won't have to look too far to meet Hostile in our society today. He gets very angry about public mention of God and finds the suggestion that there is a God in heaven who created us and to whom we are all ultimately accountable deeply offensive.

You may have noticed that many kind and respectable people are hostile when it comes to the things of God. A conversation can be quite civil until God's name is introduced. Then, it is as if a switch is triggered, and a deep hostility within the soul is opened up.

Hostile has neither the desire nor the ability to follow God's Law.

Helpless: Desire Without Ability

> I do not understand what I do. For what I want
> to do I do not do, but what I hate I do.
> (ROMANS 7:15)

In Romans 7, we meet another character whom we will call Helpless.

Helpless knows that God's Law is good. He wants to do it (vv. 17–18), but he doesn't have the ability. Helpless is a prisoner of the law of sin. It is as if he were in chains, and he cannot get free.

This leaves him feeling absolutely miserable. "What a wretched man I am!" Helpless says. "Who will rescue me from this body of death?" (v. 24).

Hopeful: Desire with Ability

> *Through Christ Jesus the law of the Spirit of life*
> *set me free from the law of sin and death.*
> *(ROMANS 8:2)*

In Romans 8, we meet a third character whom we will call Hopeful.

Paul tells Hopeful to "put to death the misdeeds of the body" (v. 13). That is precisely what Helpless could not do! But Hopeful is in an entirely different position. He has the desire to fight against sin in his life, but he also has the ability to prevail, and the reason is that the Spirit of God lives in Him.

Hopeful and Helpless face the same struggles. They feel the power of the same temptations. The difference between them lies not in the battle but in the outcome. Helpless faces inevitable defeat. Hopeful faces ultimate victory.

PEARL HARBOR:
HOPE IN AN OVERWHELMING FORCE

When Pearl Harbor was attacked on December 7, 1941, Winston Churchill was at Chequers, the British prime minister's country retreat. On hearing the news, he called President Franklin Roosevelt, who confirmed what had happened. "It's quite true," Roosevelt said. "They have attacked us at Pearl Harbor. We are all in the same boat now."

Churchill recorded his thoughts as he went to bed that night.

"No American will think it wrong of me if I proclaim that to have the United States at our side was to me the greatest joy . . . So we had won after all! Yes, after Dunkirk; after the fall of France . . . after seventeen months of lonely fighting and nineteen months of my responsibility in dire stress. We had won the war. England would live; Britain would live!

"How long the war would last or in what fashion it would end no man could tell, nor did I at this moment care . . . Many disasters, immeasurable cost and tribulation lay ahead, but there was no more doubt about the end. *All the rest was merely the proper application of overwhelming force* . . . I went to bed and slept the sleep of the saved and thankful" (emphasis added).[1]

The war would drag on for another four years. It would continue to be a bitter struggle, but even in December 1941, Churchill could say, "We had won after all." The outcome was certain.

During the London Blitz of 1940, Churchill had been "Helpless." But now he was "Hopeful." The difference lay in the involvement of an overwhelming force.

If you belong to Christ, the Holy Spirit is with you and in you. You are not Helpless, so don't talk as if you were. God has placed you in an entirely new position "in Christ." You will face the same battles as you did before, but there will be a different outcome. "Sin shall not be your master" (Romans 6:14).

IDENTIFY YOUR POSITION AND HEAR GOD'S WORD

Which of our three friends do you identify with: Hostile, Helpless, or Hopeful?

It's important to answer this question accurately, because you can't take the next step forward in your spiritual life until you know where you are.

God's Word to Hostile

If you are Hostile, God says, "I love you." As Paul wrote, "God demonstrates his own love for us in this: While we were still sinners, Christ died for us" (Romans 5:8).

God poured out His love toward us while we were still hostile toward Him. He has loved you through all your struggling, resisting, and fighting against Him. He loves you still, even in your hostility.

God offers an amnesty to those who are hostile. He invites you to lay down your arms and offers you the opportunity to repent. Repentance is giving up your resistance to God. Jesus Christ came into the world and went to the cross so that those who were once God's enemies could become His friends.

God's Word to Helpless

God's word to Helpless is quite different. He already wants to do what is right. His problem is that he doesn't have the power.

When Helpless cries out in despair, "Who will rescue me from this body of death?" God's answer is "Jesus Christ" (Romans 7:25).

The Christian life is about the power of God entering your soul to break the power that has been ruling over you. Christ will deliver you.

Come to Christ in faith. Tell Him that you cannot live this life on your own. Tell Him that you need the power of His Holy Spirit so that you will have the ability as well as the desire to live a new life. Ask and you will receive. Seek and you will find. God will give you a new name; you will no longer be Helpless; you will be Hopeful.

God's Word to Hopeful

God tells all who are Hopeful to "put to death the misdeeds of the body" by the power of the Spirit (Romans 8:13). "Start an intentional battle against sin that remains in you, Hopeful. Learn to fight, and don't ever say that you are Helpless," God is saying. "The Spirit of God is within you. Christ has put you in a position to fight and win."

Are you making the proper application of overwhelming force? Can you identify specific sins on which you are launching an intentional assault at this point in your life? Are you praying about them? Have you formed a strategy for change, knowing that the power of the Spirit has been given to you to make this possible?

Hopeful, the Spirit of God is within you. Fight!

Remember that the enemy will try to confuse you about your position. He loves to tell every Hopeful that he or she is really Helpless. Many of his greatest successes come from that kind of propaganda. So identify your position, and then follow God's instructions.

If you are Hostile, "Repent!" God's love reaches out to you.

If you are Helpless, "Come!" Christ will deliver you.

If you are Hopeful, "Fight!" The Holy Spirit is within you.

Pause for Prayer

Gracious Father,

Thank You that, through Jesus Christ, You have made a way for Your enemies to become Your friends. Thank You that Christ has come, not only to pay sin's penalty but also to break sin's power. Thank You that You have made the Christian life possible by the power of Your Spirit. Help me to make a proper application of His power in my struggles and so to prevail for Jesus' sake, amen.

Questions for Discussion

1. How does God show His love to people who are "hostile"?

2. Why is the Christian life so difficult?

3. If you are "hopeful," what are the primary battles you are fighting right now? How is it going?

4. Do you believe that God's Holy Spirit will come alongside those who feel helpless? What holds you back from believing in Jesus and asking for the help of His Spirit in your battles?

NOTE
1. Winston S. Churchill, *The Second World War* (London: The Reprint Society, 1950), 3:475–77.

THE STORY CONTINUES...

*A*LONGSIDE Paul, other apostles exercised a powerful ministry in the early days of the church. The apostle John, for example, wrote the fourth gospel and three letters that bear his name in the New Testament.

In his old age, John was imprisoned on the Isle of Patmos. While he was there, God gave him a vision of the future, which the apostle recorded in the book of Revelation.

John knew that Jesus had promised to come again. When Christ ascended, John had heard the angel confirm that Jesus would come in the same way as the apostles had seen Him go. And so He will come again—personally and visibly—and when He comes, He will bring all His people into His immediate presence.

The book of Revelation tells us how the Bible story will end. It is full of wonderful symbols that help us to grasp things that would otherwise be beyond the range of our understanding.

John saw the evil that would be unleashed across history and especially in the last days. He saw the joy of Christ's people when they are taken out of the suffering of this world and welcomed into Christ's presence. He saw the final victory of Christ when evil will be destroyed.

Then he saw the new heaven and the new earth . . .

The CITY

—**DISCOVER**—

the joys of God's new heaven and earth.

—**LEARN**—

how you can be part of God's ultimate purpose.

—**WORSHIP**—

because God will make all things new.

*T*HINK about the way a pearl necklace hangs from a woman's neck. It falls and then it rises so that the first and last pearls in the string sit next to each other, divided only by the clasp. When the clasp is undone and the necklace is stretched out, the first and last pearls seem far apart, but when they are joined by the clasp, they are brought closely together.

The Bible story begins in a garden, ends in a city, and all the way through points us to Jesus Christ. The garden and the city may seem a long way apart. But, like the pearls on the necklace, God has brought them remarkably close together.

The Bible begins with God creating the heavens and the earth. It ends with God creating a new heaven and a new earth. Everything that Adam lost will be restored and much more besides.

A NEW HEAVEN AND A NEW EARTH

Then I saw a new heaven and a new earth, for the first heaven and the first earth had passed away. (REVELATION 21:1)

We can easily understand why God would make a new earth, but why would God make a new heaven?

Before there was ever rebellion on earth, there was rebellion in heaven. Satan wanted to ascend to the throne of God, and so he was cast out. The possibility of evil existed both on the earth and in heaven.

But now John sees that the enemy will be consigned to destruction forever and that God will shape a new heaven, free not only from the presence of evil but even from its possibility.

Then John says that he saw a "new earth." "New" means that it will be wonderfully different. "Earth" means that it will be strangely familiar. The destiny of the Christian believer is not a dreamlike existence in an imaginary world. God will reshape, re-create, replenish, and renew this planet (Romans 8:21).

The joys of the new heaven and earth are beyond anything that we can imagine, but God uses two pictures to give us some inkling of what lies ahead for His people. They are the city and the garden.

JERUSALEM, JERUSALEM

> *I saw the Holy City, the new Jerusalem, coming down out of heaven from God. (21:2)*

At this point in the story, history as we know it has been brought to a close. London, Chicago, Jerusalem, Cairo, Peking, Moscow, Baghdad, Bangkok, Johannesburg, and Calcutta are all gone! The earth has been laid bare in the fervent heat of God's judgment. (See Hebrews 1:10–12 and 2 Peter 3:10.)

Now John sees a new city coming down from heaven. He immediately recognizes its skyline. Jerusalem! It was unmistakably familiar to him.

Jerusalem is full of significance in the Bible story. This was the place where God came down to meet with His people when the cloud of His presence filled the temple.

Taking the Measurements

The new city was vast. It was laid out like a square and measured 12,000 stadia (Revelation 21:16). That's 1,400 miles, about the distance from New York to Houston. The area covered by the city would be about three-quarters the size of America or five times the size of Great Britain. It was absolutely overwhelming.

John had already seen that God's people are more than anyone could number. Now God was communicating that He has a vast city for this vast crowd. He has a place for every one of His people.

The measurements of the city are given in three dimensions. It is "as wide and high as it is long" (v. 16) In other words, it is a perfect cube.

Seeing a Holy Place

John would have seen the significance of this immediately. The Most Holy Place in the temple, where God met with His people was also a perfect cube, thirty feet long, thirty feet wide, and thirty feet high (1 Kings 6:20).

The old city had a holy place, where the presence of God came down. The new city is a holy place, where God's presence will remain. In the old Jerusalem, one room was filled with His glory. In the New Jerusalem, the whole city will be filled with His glory, and a vast crowd of men and women, more than anyone could number, will live in God's presence.

PARADISE RESTORED: THE GARDEN

*Then the angel showed me the river of the water
of life . . . . On each side of the river stood the
tree of life, bearing twelve crops of fruit, yielding
its fruit every month. (22:1–2)*

A New Garden

Up to this point in the vision, John has viewed the New
Jerusalem from the outside. But now, he is invited to come
inside. As he enters, the picture changes and, no doubt to
his absolute astonishment, John sees a garden!

The Bible story began in a garden and now, at the end of
the Bible story, this paradise is restored. But notice that
there is no "tree of the knowledge of good and evil" in
God's new garden city. Evil can no longer be known there.
This garden is free not only from the presence of evil, but
even from its possibility.

The Tree of Life

In the new garden, God's people have access to the Tree of
Life, which bears twelve different crops of fruit, ready to
pick every month. The variety of fruit speaks of the riches
of life, continually replenished in the presence of God.

The pleasures of God's new garden city will surpass anything Adam knew in the Garden of Eden. You will taste fruits Adam never tasted and enjoy pleasures Adam never knew.

SERVING AND REIGNING

His servants will serve him . . . . They will reign for ever and ever. (22:3, 5)

In the first garden, Adam served God by ruling or reigning over the animal kingdom. He stood in authority over them. But when the serpent came, he did not maintain his rule.

But now God's people are restored to a position of serving and reigning. Thankfully, this does not mean that we will all have jobs in government administration!

When God speaks about us reigning, He is telling us that life will be ordered and brought under your control. You will no longer be subject to the tyranny of time, piles of paperwork, and all that goes with it. You will no longer be swept away by unpredictable tides of emotion, deceptions of the mind, or impulses of the will. You will no longer endure dysfunctional relationships, and you will no longer be subject to danger or death.

Your life will be ordered, your work fulfilled, and your relationships whole. Life itself will be brought under your control, and you will be free to fulfill all the purposes of God.

ENJOYING THE PRESENCE OF GOD

> *The throne of God and of the Lamb will be in the city, and his servants will serve him. They will see his face. (22:3–4)*

God's presence in this city is its greatest blessing. In the Garden of Eden, God came down as a visitor and made Himself known. He did not impose Himself on the man and the woman, but gave them the opportunity of choosing a relationship of faith and obedience with Him.

But now God has gathered a vast community of people who have come to love Him freely. So God is no longer a visitor. His throne comes down into the city so that God's people may live in His presence and enjoy Him forever. "Now the dwelling of God is with men" (21:3).

THE GREAT INVITATION

> *The Spirit and the bride say, "Come!" (22:17)*

John saw twelve gates into God's garden city. There were three on each side, indicating that people would come from the north, south, east, and west into it (21:12–13).

John saw an angel at each gate (21:12). At the beginning of the Bible story, the cherubim and a flaming sword guarded the entrance to the Tree of Life. But there is no flaming sword now. Jesus Christ has come, and the sword of God's judgment has been broken on Him. Now the angels stand by the gates, not to forbid entrance but to provide a welcome for all who will come.

The Lord Jesus Christ has opened up the way to everlasting life for you. He offers all this to you, but you must come! Enter, by repentance and faith, into what Jesus has opened up for you. Come and receive the life that He offers to you. Come to Him, because His people will enter into this marvelous city.

The Spirit and the bride invite you to come (22:17). The bride is the church. If you have not yet come to faith in Jesus Christ, it is more than likely that there is a Christian somewhere who has been praying and longing that you will do so. It is my privilege to speak for the bride and invite you to come.

The Holy Spirit also says, "Come." God wants you to be part of this, and He invites you. Do not stand at a distance from the priceless gift He offers to you. Come!

PHOTOGRAPHS AND MEMORIES

I'm grateful that my wife, Karen, enjoys putting photograph albums together. They are a wonderful record of our lives. We all experience life in different places at different moments of time. When I look through the photograph album, I remember, "Yes, I was there then."

As you read the end of this book, you are in a particular place, at a moment in time. You know yourself to be here, now.

If you have come to Christ, the moment will come when you will know yourself to be there. And when you are there, you will be there forever.

Pause for Prayer

Gracious Lord,

I come to receive by faith what You offer me in Jesus Christ. I ask that You will make me a citizen of Your kingdom, and that one day Christ will lead me into the place He is preparing for all His people.

Thank You that this is His promise for all who believe, and therefore that it is His promise to me. Help me to live for Your glory until that day dawns, in Jesus' name, amen.

Questions for Discussion

1. Which characteristics of God's Garden City appeal to you most?

2. On what basis will people be allowed or denied access to the New Jerusalem?

3. What difference can the Christian's hope make to the reality of daily life now?

4. What is the most important thing God has taught you through this book? What difference can this make to your life?

Bible Study Helps by Moody Press

Unlocking the Bible Story
Volume 3 & 4

There are many people who know stories from the Bible, but
they have not grasped the story of the Bible.

Unlocking the Bible Story will
help you:

Discover - the Bible as one whole
marvelous story
Learn - the major themes with the
chapter titled with one word taken
from the Bible
Worship - as the whole Bible
revolves around one central focus,
our Lord Jesus Christ

ISBN: 0-8024-6545-5 Hardback   *Volume 3 - New Testament Pt. 3*
ISBN: 0-8024-6546-3 Hardback   *Volume 4 - New Testament Pt. 4*

MOODY
The Name You Can Trust
1-800-678-8812 **www.MoodyPress.org**

Bible Study Helps by Moody Press

Unlocking the Bible Story
Volume 1 & 2

"This is a satisfying and insightful overview of Scripture that tells "the old, old story" in a fascinating way. Even seasoned Bible students will find their eyes opened and their hearts warmed as they read it."

Warren Wiersbe Author and Conference Speaker

For all who are wondering how the pieces fit into the jigsaw of God's revelation, Colin Smith has provided an answer, which is refreshingly simple, Biblically accurate and will prove phenomenally helpful to the serious Bible student and the new beginner alike.

Alister Begg, Senior Pastor, Parkside Church

Colin Smith's Unlocking the Bible Story *is a significant work. In fact I'm convinced it will make a lasting contribution to God's people regardless of age or ethnicity.*

Dr. Gregory L. Waybright, President Trinity International University

ISBN: 0-8024-6543-9   **Hardback**   *Volume 1 - Old Testament Pt. 1*
ISBN: 0-8024-6544-7   **Hardback**   *Volume 2 - Old Testament Pt. 2*

Find out More on Colin Smith's Unlocking the Bible web site

Unlocking the Bible web site was created to help you discover the Bible so that you may know God...and there's nothing greater than that.

JOIN online community discussions
HEAR Pastor Colin's weekly radio program
READ through the Bible

Unlocking the Bible is here to help you discover the whole Bible story. We want to help you discover the breathtaking sweep of God's plan as it is unfolded in the Bible story, which begins in a garden and ends in a city, and all the way through is about Jesus Christ.

www.unlockingthebible.org